Humorous Quotations

Humorous Quotations

The wit and wisdom of the world's funniest people

ARCTURUS

ARCTURUS

This edition published in 2013 by Arcturus Publishing Limited
26/27 Bickels Yard, 151–153 Bermondsey Street,
London SE1 3HA

ISBN: 978-1-78212-449-8
AD002359EN

Printed in China

Contents

Humorous Quotations

Hollywood Hogwash

I learned a long time ago in Hollywood that the only person I should vote for is myself.

Jack Nicholson, US actor

In my mind, I've always been an A-list Hollywood superstar. Y'all just didn't know yet.

Will Smith, US actor

Carpe per diem – seize the cheque.

Robin Williams, US comedian

I have an everyday religion that works for me. Love yourself first, and everything else falls into line.

Lucille Ball, US comedian

The movies are the only business where you can go out front and applaud yourself.

Will Rogers, US actor

Man to John Wayne while he is watching the All Ireland Hurling semi-final:

Hey, John, how would you like to be out there with a stick yourself?

John Wayne:

Well, I sure as hell wouldn't like to be out there without one!

Hollywood is a place where a man can get stabbed in the back while climbing a ladder.

William Faulkner, US writer

Hollywood is a place where they'll pay you a thousand dollars for a kiss and fifty cents for your soul.

Marilyn Monroe, US actress

Being rich is better than being poor, if only for financial reasons.

Woody Allen, US writer-director

If my films don't show a profit, I know I'm doing something right.

Woody Allen, US writer-director

Dogs got personality. Personality goes a long way.

Quentin Tarantino, US director

There's only one thing that can kill the movies, and that's education.

Will Rogers, US actor

There are a lot of things I learned from animals. One was that they couldn't hiss or boo me.

James Dean, US actor

Dogs never bite me. Just humans.

Marilyn Monroe, US actress

Why can't a woman be more like a dog, huh? So sweet, loving, attentive.

Kirk Douglas, US actor

In Hollywood, you play a mom, and the next thing you know, you're on *The Golden Girls*. They age you so fast.

Gabrielle Union, US actress

I really want to play Princess Leia. Stick some big pastries on my head. Now that would be interesting!

Ewan McGregor, Scottish actor

I don't mind that I'm fat. You still get the same money.

Marlon Brando, US actor

Women need a reason to have sex – men just need a place.

Billy Crystal, US actor

In Hollywood, the women are all peaches. It makes one long for an apple occasionally.

W. Somerset Maugham, British writer

Hosting the Oscars is much like making love to a woman. It's something I only get to do when Billy Crystal is out of town.

Steve Martin, US comedian

Shoot a few scenes out of focus. I want to win the foreign film award.

Billy Wilder, Austrian screenwriter and director

I love Marlon Brando. Never seen him bad, just less good.

Lee Marvin, US actor

In Hollywood, brides keep the bouquets and throw away the groom.

Groucho Marx, US comedian

I'm just a lucky slob from Ohio who happened to be in the right place at the right time.

Clark Gable, US actor

A successful man is one who makes more money than his wife can spend. A successful woman is one who can find such a man.

Lana Turner, US actress

For twenty-four years I've been in love with the same woman. If my wife ever finds out, she'll kill me.

Henny Youngman, British-American comedian

Sticking with a marriage. That's true grit, man.

Jeff Bridges, US actor

Here's to our wives and girlfriends ... may they never meet!

Groucho Marx, US comedian

I was always a character actor. I just looked like Little Red Riding Hood.

Paul Newman, US actor

Even if I set out to make a film about a fillet of sole, it would be about me.

Federico Fellini, Italian director

I was in a bar and I said to a friend, 'You know, we've become those 40-year-old guys we used to look at and say, "Isn't it sad?"'

George Clooney, US actor

When an actor comes to me and wants to discuss his character, I say, 'It's in the script.' If he says, 'But what's my motivation?,' I say, 'Your salary.'

Alfred Hitchcock, English director

25

Hollywood Hogwash

I wouldn't be caught dead marrying a woman old enough to be my wife.

Tony Curtis, US actor

In Hollywood, an equitable divorce settlement means each party getting fifty per cent of publicity.

Lauren Bacall, US actress

Hollywood is a place where they place you under contract instead of under observation.

Walter Winchell, US columnist

Well, you know what they say in Hollywood – the most important thing is being sincere, even if you have to fake it.

Cesar Romero, US actor

I hate television. I hate it as much as peanuts. But I can't stop eating peanuts.

Orson Welles, US director

For me, the cinema is not a slice of life, but a piece of cake.

Alfred Hitchcock, English director

Donuts - is there anything they can't do?

Homer Simpson, cartoon character

The most important question in American cinema, I've learned, is 'When is lunch?'

Tommy Lee Jones, US actor

Ever wonder if illiterate people get the full effect of alphabet soup?

John Mendoza, US comedian

Talking business disgusts me. If you want to talk business, call my disgusting personal manager.

Sylvester Stallone, US actor

Man invented language to satisfy his deep need to complain.

Lily Tomlin, US actress

I only sound intelligent when there's a good scriptwriter around.

Christian Bale, English actor

People think I have an interesting walk. Hell, I am just trying to hold my gut in.

Robert Mitchum, US actor

The average Hollywood film star's ambition is to be admired by an American, courted by an Italian, married to an Englishman and have a French boyfriend.

Katharine Hepburn, US actress

There's an old saying in Hollywood: It's not the length of your film, it's how you use it.

Ben Stiller, US actor

Hollywood Hogwash

It's not so much knowing when to speak ... but when to pause.

Jack Benny, US comedian

The length of a film should be directly related to the endurance of the human bladder.

Alfred Hitchcock, English director

Talk low, talk slow and don't say too much.

John Wayne's recipe for success

I know very little about acting. I'm just an incredibly gifted faker.

Robert Downey, Jr., US actor

Man does not control his own fate. The women in his life do that for him.

Groucho Marx, US comedian

Never comment on a woman's rear end. Never use the words 'large' or 'size' with 'rear end'. Never. Avoid the area altogether. Trust me.

Tim Allen, US comedian

I didn't discover curves; I only uncovered them.

Mae West, US actress

Hollywood Hogwash

Women are like cars:
we all want a Ferrari,
sometimes want a pick-up
truck, and end up with a
station wagon.

Tim Allen, US comedian

*She got her looks
from her father. He's
a plastic surgeon.*

Groucho Marx, US comedian

Girls have an unfair advantage over men: if they can't get what they want by being smart, they can get it by being dumb.

Yul Brynner, US actor

Give me a couple of years, and I'll make that actress an overnight success.

Samuel Goldwyn, US film producer

Hollywood Hogwash

Although it wasn't that easy to do, it was wonderful working with John Wayne.

Robert Duvall, US actor

It's said in Hollywood that you should always forgive your enemies - because you never know when you'll have to work with them.

Lana Turner, US actress

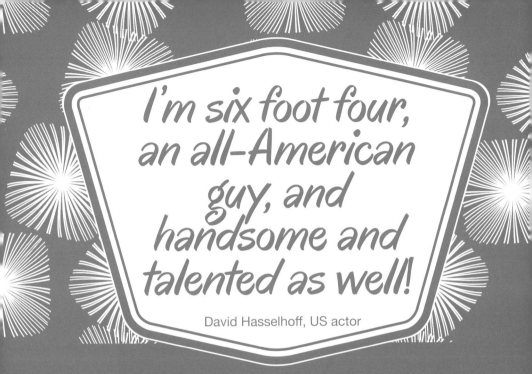

I'm six foot four, an all-American guy, and handsome and talented as well!

David Hasselhoff, US actor

I stopped believing in Santa Claus when I was six. Mother took me to see him in a department store and he asked for my autograph.

Shirley Temple, US actress

I only take Viagra when I'm with more than one woman.

Jack Nicholson, US actor

Just let the wardrobe do the acting.

Jack Nicholson, US actor

Being born with a pair of beady eyes was the best thing that ever happened to me.

Lee van Cleef, US actor

Where is Hollywood located? Chiefly between the ears. In that part of the American brain lately vacated by God.

Erica Jong, US writer

They say marriages are made in heaven. But so is thunder and lightning.

Clint Eastwood, US actor

I see you're a man with ideals. I better be going before you've still got them.

Mae West, US actress

If women ran the world we wouldn't have wars, just intense negotiations every twenty-eight days.

Robin Williams,
US comedian

If I had to live my life again, I'd make the same mistakes, only sooner.

Tallulah Bankhead, US actress

Hollywood Hogwash

I'm not sure that acting is something for a grown man to be doing.

Steve McQueen, US actor

The term 'serious actor' is kind of an oxymoron, isn't it? Like 'Republican party' or 'airplane food'.

Johnny Depp, US actor

One morning I shot an elephant in my pajamas. How he got into my pajamas I'll never know.

Groucho Marx, US comedian

If you're going to be subtle in a movie, make it extremely obvious.

Billy Wilder, Austrian screenwriter and director

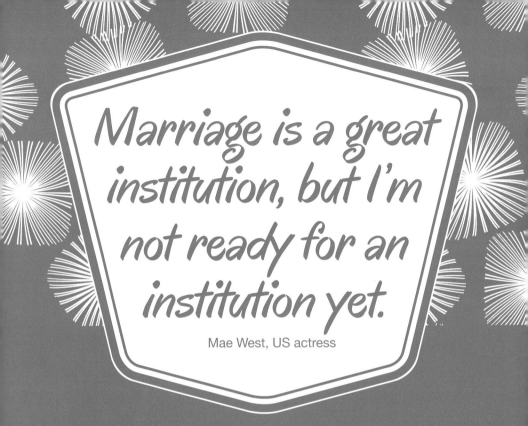

Marriage is a great institution, but I'm not ready for an institution yet.

Mae West, US actress

I love Mickey Mouse more than any woman I have ever known.

Walt Disney, US movie mogul

Eighty per cent of married men cheat in America; the rest cheat in Europe.

Jackie Mason, US comedian

An associate producer is the only guy in Hollywood who will associate with a producer.

Fred Allen, US comedian

Hollywood Hogwash

Marriage requires a special talent like acting. Monogamy requires genius.

Warren Beatty, US actor

You can take all the sincerity in Hollywood, place it in the navel of a fruit fly and still have room enough for three caraway seeds and a producer's heart.

Fred Allen, US comedian

My driving abilities from Mexico have helped me get through Hollywood.

Salma Hayek, Mexican-American actress

Stardom isn't a profession, it's an accident.

Lauren Bacall, US actress

The road to success is always under construction

Lily Tomlin, US actress

Hollywood Hogwash

First you forget names, then you forget faces. Next you forget to pull your zipper up and finally you forget to pull it down.

George Burns, US comedian

In Hollywood now when people die they don't say, 'Did he leave a will?' but 'Did he leave a diary?'

Liza Minnelli, US actress and singer

I don't feel old. I don't feel anything till noon. That's when it's time for my nap

Bob Hope, US comedian

One thing about being successful is that I stopped being afraid of dying. Once you're a star you're dead already. You're embalmed.

Dustin Hoffman, US actor

If at first you don't succeed, try again. Then quit. There's no use being a damn fool about it.

W. C. Fields, US comedian

You're not a star until they can spell your name in Karachi.

Humphrey Bogart, US actor

My wife Mary and I have been married for forty-seven years and not once have we had an argument serious enough to consider divorce; murder, yes, but divorce, never.

Jack Benny, US comedian

If I ever lose a role because of my tattoos, I'll quit Hollywood and go to work at Costco.

Megan Fox, US actress

Why don't you put that in the headline: 'He Only Did Three With Doris!' Set a lot of people straight.

Rock Hudson, US actor, on his films with Doris Day

In Hollywood it seems that you're considered gay until proven otherwise.

Ryan Seacrest, US TV presenter and producer

A star on a movie set is like a time bomb. That bomb has got to be defused so people can approach it without fear.

Jack Nicholson, US actor

Hollywood is where they shoot too many films and not enough actors.

Walter Winchell, US columnist

I only direct in self-defense.

Mel Brooks, US director

I was street smart, but unfortunately the street was Rodeo Drive.

Carrie Fisher, US actress

Every actor in his heart believes everything bad that's printed about him.

Orson Welles, US director

If my books had been any worse, I should not have been invited to Hollywood, and if they had been any better, I should not have come.

Raymond Chandler, US writer

Hollywood Hogwash

A rich man is nothing but a poor man with money.

W. C. Fields, US comedian

I made more lousy pictures than any actor in history.

Humphrey Bogart, US actor

He who hesitates is poor.

Mel Brooks, US director

I've played three presidents, three saints and two geniuses - and that's probably enough for any man.

Charlton Heston, US actor

How can a president not be an actor?

Ronald Reagan, US President

Most beautiful dumb girls think they're smart and get away with it because other people, on the whole, aren't much smarter.

Louise Brooks, US actress

I just found out about ten days ago that I live 300 yards from Britney Spears ... now I have to move.

George Clooney, US actor

In Hollywood, a marriage is a success if it outlasts milk.

Rita Rudner, US comedian

We all respect sincerity in our friends and acquaintances, but Hollywood is willing to pay for it.

Hattie McDaniel, US actress

Hollywood didn't kill Marilyn Monroe, it's the Marilyn Monroes who are killing Hollywood.

Billy Wilder, Austrian screenwriter and director

If God doesn't destroy Hollywood Boulevard, he owes Sodom and Gomorrah an apology.

Jay Leno, US comedian and chat show host

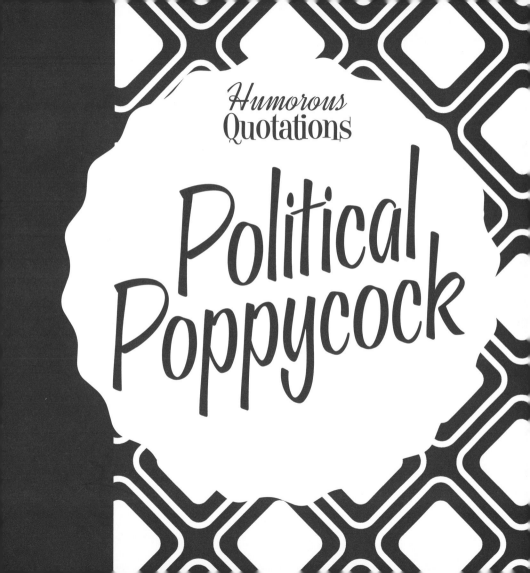

Humorous
Quotations

Political
Poppycock

Political Poppycock

My job is to, like, think beyond the immediate.

George W. Bush, US President

A fool and his money are soon elected.

Will Rogers, US actor

America can't beat anyone anymore.

George Clooney, US actor

One of the penalties for refusing to participate in politics is that you end up being governed by your inferiors.

Plato, Greek philosopher

My brother Bob doesn't want to be in government - he promised Dad he'd go straight.

John F. Kennedy, US President

Crime does not pay ... as much as politics.

Alfred E. Newman, mascot of *Mad* magazine

I think JR would make a better President than the one we have now.

Larry Hagman, US actor

Any American who is prepared to run for president should automatically, by definition, be disqualified from ever doing so.

Gore Vidal, US writer

Without censorship things can get terribly confused in the public mind.

General William Westmoreland during the Vietnam war, US President

Politics is too serious a matter to be left to the politicians.

Charles de Gaulle, French President

Ask not what you can do for your country. Ask what's for lunch.

Orson Welles, US director

In order to become the master, the politician poses as the servant.

Charles de Gaulle, French President

Political Poppycock

Some newspapers are fit only to line the bottom of bird cages.

Spiro T. Agnew, US Vice President

Freedom of the press is guaranteed only to those who own one.

A. J. Liebling, US journalist

72

To the world I am America.

Charlton Heston, US actor

Thank you, your Holiness. Awesome speech.

George W. Bush, US President to Pope Benedict

Politics is the entertainment branch of industry.

Frank Zappa, US musician

I was recently on a tour of Latin America, and the only regret I have was that I didn't study Latin harder in school so I could converse with those people.

Dan Quayle, US Vice President

Republicans understand the importance of bondage between a mother and child.

Dan Quayle, US Vice President

When buying and selling are controlled by legislation, the first things to be bought and sold are legislators.

P. J. O'Rourke, US political satirist

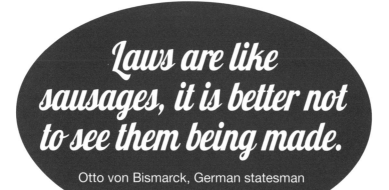

Laws are like sausages, it is better not to see them being made.

Otto von Bismarck, German statesman

I predict, sir, that you will die either by hanging or of some vile disease.

William Gladstone,
British Liberal politician

That all depends, sir, upon whether I embrace your principles or your mistress.

Benjamin Disraeli, British Prime Minister

Behind every successful man is a surprised woman.

Mary Pearson, wife of Lester Pearson, Canadian Prime Minister

It has been said that politics is the second oldest profession. I have learned that it bears a striking resemblance to the first.

Ronald Reagan, US President

The people of England are never so happy as when you tell them they are ruined.

Arthur Murphy, Irish writer

The best argument against democracy is a five-minute conversation with the average voter.

Winston Churchill, British Prime Minister

It is better to remain silent and be thought a fool than to speak and remove all doubt.

Abraham Lincoln, US President

Suppose you were an idiot, and suppose you were a member of Congress; but I repeat myself.

Mark Twain, US writer

The Oval Office is the kind of place where people stand outside, they're getting ready to come in and tell me what for, and they walk in and get overwhelmed in the atmosphere, and they say, man, you're looking pretty.

George W. Bush, US President

An ideal form of government is democracy tempered with assassination.

Voltaire, French writer

See, I love to bring people into the Oval Office and say, this is where I office.

George W. Bush, US President

I'll be long gone before some smart person ever figures out what happened inside this Oval Office.

George W. Bush, US President

He says he works out because it clears his mind. Sometimes just a little too much.

Jay Leno, US comedian and chat show host, on George W. Bush

If Khrushchev had been assassinated instead of Kennedy do you think Mr Onassis would have married Mrs Khrushchev?

Henry Kissinger, US diplomat on the beauty of Jackie Kennedy

Democracy is the process by which people choose the man who'll get the blame.

Bertrand Russell, British philosopher

Never murder a man when he's busy committing suicide.

Woodrow Wilson, US President

It is forbidden to kill; therefore all murderers are punished unless they kill in large numbers and to the sound of trumpets.

Voltaire, French writer

If God had intended us not to eat animals, how come He made them out of meat?

Sarah Palin, US politician

I've noticed that everyone who is for abortion has already been born.

Ronald Reagan, US President

Never do today what you can do tomorrow. Something may occur to make you regret your premature action.

Aaron Burr, US Vice President

I have left orders to be awakened at any time during national emergency, even if I'm in a cabinet meeting.

Ronald Reagan, US President

Things are more like they are now than they ever were before.

Dwight D. Eisenhower, US President

It is remarkable how easily children and grown-ups adapt to living in a dictatorship organized by lunatics.

A. N. Wilson, English writer

Verbosity leads to unclear, inarticulate things.

Dan Quayle, US Vice President

In Downing Street they call me 'Boss'.

Tony Blair, British Prime Minister

Frankly, I don't mind not being President. I just mind that someone else is.

Edward Kennedy, US senator

There is something about the outside of a horse that is good for the inside of a man.

Winston Churchill, British Prime Minister

A sheep in sheep's clothing... a modest man with much to be modest about.

Winston Churchill, British Prime Minister on rival British politician Clement Attlee

Only two things are necessary to keep one's wife happy. One is to let her think she is having her own way, and the other is to let her have it.

Lyndon B. Johnson, US President

My wife and I tried two or three times in the last few years to have breakfast together, but it was so disagreeable we had to stop.

Winston Churchill, British Prime Minister

Lady Astor to Winston Churchill:

Sir, if you were my husband, I would poison your drink.

Churchill in reponse:

Madam, if you were my wife, I would drink it.

He doesn't dye
his hair,
he bleaches
his face.

Johnny Carson, US chat show host,
on Ronald Reagan

I believe there is something out
there watching us. Unfortunately,
it's the government.

Woody Allen, US writer-director

If ignorance goes to $40 a barrel, I want drilling rights to George Bush's head.

Jim Hightower, US liberal political activist,
about George Bush, Sr

Half of the American people have never read a newspaper. Half never voted for President. One hopes it is the same half.

Gore Vidal, US writer

Americans have different ways of saying things. They say 'elevator', we say 'lift' ... they say, 'President', we say, 'stupid psychopath'.

Alexei Sayle, British comedian

Politics is the art of looking for trouble, finding it everywhere, diagnosing it incorrectly and applying the wrong remedies.

Groucho Marx, US comedian

I'm not worried about the deficit. It's big enough to take care of itself.

Ronald Reagan, US President

I don't make predictions. I never have and never will.

Tony Blair, British Prime Minister

The inherent vice of capitalism is the unequal sharing of blessings; the inherent virtue of socialism is the equal sharing of miseries.

Winston Churchill, British Prime Minister

To cure the British disease with socialism was like trying to cure leukaemia with leeches.

Margaret Thatcher, British Prime Minister

The meek will inherit the earth — but not the mineral rights.

J. Paul Getty, US industrialist

These capitalists generally act harmoniously, and in concert, to fleece the people

Abraham Lincoln, US President

Glory is fleeting, but obscurity is forever.

Napoleon Bonaparte, French dictator

Television has made dictatorship impossible but democracy unbearable.

Shimon Peres, Israeli President

I've always thought that underpopulated countries in Africa are vastly under-polluted.

Lawrence Summers, US economist, explaining why we should export toxic waste to Third World countries

Democracy means simply the bludgeoning of the people by the people for the people.

Oscar Wilde, Irish writer

Nagging is the repetition of unpalatable truths.

Baroness Edith Summerskill, British politician

Amigo! Amigo!

George W. Bush, US President, calling out to Italian Prime Minister Silvio Berlusconi in Spanish

Republicans have been accused of abandoning the poor. It's the other way around. They never vote for us.

Dan Quayle, US Vice President

I'm honoured to shake the hand of a brave Iraqi citizen who had his hand cut off by Saddam Hussein.

George W. Bush, US President

Those who stand for nothing fall for anything.

Alexander Hamilton, US Founding Father

The day I made that statement, about inventing the internet, I was tired because I'd been up all night inventing the camcorder.

Al Gore, US Vice President

When I am right, I get angry. Churchill gets angry when he is wrong. We are angry at each other much of the time.

French President Charles de Gaulle on British PM Winston Churchill

The reason there are two Senators for each state is so that one can be the designated driver.

Jay Leno, US comedian and chat show host

You want a friend in Washington? Get a dog.

Harry S. Truman, US President

A government survey showed the Prime Minister was doing the work of two men - Laurel and Hardy.

Ronnie Corbett, British comedian

The difference between a democracy and a dictatorship is that in a democracy you vote first and take orders later; in a dictatorship you don't have to waste your time voting.

Charles Bukowski, US writer

Do you realize the responsibility I carry? I'm the only person standing between Richard Nixon and the White House.

John F. Kennedy, US President

If voting changed anything, they'd make it illegal.

Emma Goldman, US anarchist

Hell, I never vote
for anybody,
I always vote
against.

W. C. Fields, US comedian

Paul Revere was warning the British about gun control, and George Washington apparently was crossing the Delaware to bomb an abortion clinic.

Bill Maher, US comedian, on Sarah Palin's view of history

The President has kept all the promises he intended to keep.

George Stephanopolous, US political advisor

I stand by all the mis-statements that I've made.

Dan Quayle, US Vice President

A leader is a dealer in hope.

Napoleon Bonaparte, French dictator

A throne is only a bench covered in velvet.

Napoleon Bonaparte, French dictator

War does not determine who is right - only who is left.

Bertrand Russell, British philosopher

When the rich wage war, it's the poor who die.

Jean-Paul Sartre, French philosopher

We are going to have peace even if we have to fight for it.

Dwight D. Eisenhower, US President

In Mexico, an air-conditioner is called 'a politician' because it makes a lot of noise but doesn't work very well.

Len Deighton, British writer

The function of socialism is to raise suffering to a higher level.

Norman Mailer, US writer

War is only a cowardly escape from the problems of peace.

Thomas Mann, German writer

Sweat saves blood.

Erwin Rommel, German Field Marshal

Democracy is a pathetic belief in the collective wisdom of individual ignorance.

H. L. Mencken, US journalist

An intellectual is a man who doesn't know how to park his bike.

Spiro T. Agnew, US Vice President

I have seen three emperors in their nakedness, and the sight was not inspiring.

Otto von Bismarck, German statesman

A mere 40 years ago, beach volleyball was just beginning. No bureaucrat would have invented it, and that's what freedom is all about.

Newt Gingrich, US politician

I think it's a pity there isn't a hell for him to go to.

Christopher Hitchens, US journalist and atheist, on his long-time sparring partner Reverend Jerry Falwell

Tact is the ability to tell someone to go to hell in such a way that they look forward to the trip.

Winston Churchill, British Prime Minister

I believe Ronald Reagan can make this country what it once was ... a large Arctic region covered with ice.

Robin Williams, US comedian

You have to remember one thing about the will of the people: it wasn't that long ago that we were swept away by the Macarena.

Jon Stewart, US comedian

Being President is like running a cemetery: you've got a lot of people under you and nobody's listening.

Bill Clinton, US President

Too bad that all the people who know how to run the country are busy driving taxicabs and cutting hair.

George Burns, US comedian

Those who cast votes decide nothing. Those who count the votes decide everything.

Joseph Stalin, Soviet Union dictator

The oppressed are allowed once every few years to decide which particular representatives of the oppressing class are to represent and repress them.

Karl Marx, German political philosopher

A dictatorship would be a heck of a lot easier, there's no question about it.

George W. Bush, US President

How can you govern a country which has 246 varieties of cheese?

Charles de Gaulle, French President

Political Poppycock

I have never been hurt by what I have not said.

Calvin Coolidge, US President

Being the Russian leader in the Kremlin, you never know if someone's tape recording what you say.

Richard Nixon, US President

If they put the federal government in charge of the Sahara Desert, there'd be a shortage of sand in five years.

Milton Friedman, US economist

Vote: the instrument and symbol of a freeman's power to make a fool of himself and a wreck of his country.

Ambrose Bierce, *The Devil's Dictionary*

Being president is like being a jackass in a hailstorm. There's nothing to do but to stand there and take it.

Lyndon B. Johnson, US President

An empty stomach is not a good political adviser.

Albert Einstein, German physicist

Blessed are the young for they shall inherit the national debt.

Herbert Hoover, US President

When a big wind sweeps across America, there isn't a building left standing: the southern states must have been built by the first two little piggies.

Dara Ó Briain, Irish comedian

In America the young are always ready to give to those who are older than themselves the full benefits of their inexperience.

Oscar Wilde, Irish writer

Political Poppycock

I'm undaunted in my quest to amuse myself by constantly changing my hair.

Hillary Clinton, US Secretary of State

You show people what you're willing to fight for when you fight your friends.

Hillary Clinton, US Secretary of State

Recession is when a neighbour loses his job. Depression is when you lose yours.

Ronald Reagan, US President

Civilization is unbearable, but it is less unbearable at the top.

Timothy Leary, US psychologist and writer

America is the
only country that went from
barbarism to decadence
without civilization
in between.

Oscar Wilde, Irish writer

*Patriotism is, fundamentally, a
conviction that a particular country
is the best in the world because you
were born in it....*

George Bernard Shaw, Irish playwright

Although prepared for martyrdom,
I preferred that it be postponed.

Winston Churchill, British Prime Minister

*Forgive your
enemies, but never
forget their names.*

John F. Kennedy, US President

*I have a very strict gun control
policy: if there's a gun around,
I want to be in control of it.*

Clint Eastwood, US actor

Harold Wilson is going round and round the country stirring up apathy.

William Whitelaw, British Conservative politician,
on Labour's leader

Mrs Thatcher tells us she has given the French President a piece of her mind ... not a gift I would receive with alacrity.

Denis Healey, British Labour politician

Humorous
Quotations

Literary
Levity

A poet can survive everything but a misprint.

Oscar Wilde, Irish writer

Be careful about reading health
books. You may die of a misprint.

I'm quite illiterate, but I read a lot.

J. D. Salinger, US writer

Brevity is the soul of wit.

William Shakespeare, English playwright

I'm writing a book. I've got the page numbers done.

Steven Wright, US comedian

Work is the curse of the drinking classes.

Oscar Wilde, Irish writer

I've always believed in writing without a collaborator, because where two people are writing the same book, each believes he gets all the worry and only half the royalties.

Agatha Christie, British writer

Always do sober what you said you'd do drunk. That will teach you to keep your mouth shut.

Ernest Hemingway, US writer

I drink therefore I am.

W. C. Fields, US comedian

My favourite words are 'cheque' and 'enclosed'.

Dorothy Parker, US writer

According to New York publishers, Bill Clinton will get more money for his book than Hillary Clinton got for hers. Well, duh. At least his book has some sex in it.

Jay Leno, US comedian and chat show host

A pedestrian is a man in danger of his life. A walker is a man in possession of his soul.

David McCord, US poet

Salary is no object; I want only enough to keep body and soul apart.

Dorothy Parker, US writer

Literary Levity

Man – a creature created at the end of a work week when God was tired.

Mark Twain, US writer

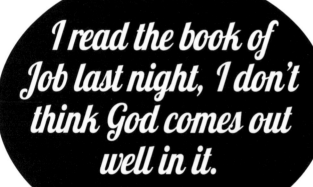

I read the book of Job last night, I don't think God comes out well in it.

Virginia Woolf, English writer

The Irish gave the bagpipes to the Scots as a joke, but the Scots haven't seen the joke yet.

Oliver Herford, US writer

Practically everybody in New York has half a mind to write a book, and does.

Groucho Marx, US comedian

Better sleep with a sober cannibal than a drunken Christian.

Herman Melville, US writer

He who hesitates is sometimes saved.

James Thurber, US writer

Sometimes I lie awake at night, and I ask, 'Where have I gone wrong?' Then a voice says to me, 'This is going to take more than one night.'

Charles Schulz's alter ego, Charlie Brown, in *Peanuts*

It is better to have loafed and lost, than never to have loafed at all.

James Thurber, US writer

Some people say that I must be a horrible person, but that's not true. I have the heart of a young boy - in a jar on my desk!

Stephen King, US writer

I don't care what is written about me so long as it isn't true.

Dorothy Parker, US writer

It usually takes more than three weeks to prepare a good impromptu speech.

Mark Twain, US writer

A smile is the chosen vehicle of all ambiguities.

Herman Melville, US writer

I cannot speak well enough to be unintelligible.

Jane Austen, British author

A banker is a fellow who lends you his umbrella when the sun is shining, but wants it back the minute it begins to rain.

Mark Twain, US writer

We do have a zeal for laughter in most situations, give or take a dentist.

Joseph Heller, US author

Goddam money. It always ends up making you blue as hell.

J. D. Salinger, US writer

Right now it's only a notion, but I think I can get the money to make it into a concept, and later turn it into an idea.

Woody Allen, US writer-director

You see a lot of smart guys with dumb women, but you hardly ever see a smart woman with a dumb guy.

Erica Jong, US writer

The man who does not read has no advantage over the man who cannot read.

Mark Twain, US writer

Lead us not into temptation. Just tell us where it is; we'll go find it.

Sam Levenson, US writer

An intellectual is a man who takes more words than necessary to tell more than he knows.

Dwight D. Eisenhower, US President

Never eat at a place called Mom's. Never play cards with a man called Doc.

Edward Abbey, US writer

There is no exception to the rule that every rule has an exception.

James Thurber, US writer

Men do not quit playing around because they grow old; they grow old because they quit playing around.

Oliver Wendell Holmes, US writer

Hell hath no fury like a hustler with a literary agent.

Frank Sinatra, US singer

> *When a man steals your wife, there is no better revenge than to let him keep her.*
>
> Sacha Guitry, French writer

> Politics is not a bad profession. If you succeed there are many rewards; if you disgrace yourself you can always write a book.
>
> Ronald Reagan, US President

When the situation is hopeless, there's nothing to worry about.

Edward Abbey, US writer

When I die, I'm leaving my body to science fiction.

Steven Wright, US comedian

God is a comedian with an audience too afraid to laugh.

Voltaire, French writer

What other culture could have produced someone like Hemingway and not seen the joke?

Gore Vidal, US writer

We are masters of the unsaid words, but slaves of those we let slip out.

Winston Churchill, British Prime Minister

Writing criticism is to writing fiction and poetry as hugging the shore is to sailing in the open sea.

John Updike, US writer

Bigamy is having one wife too many. Monogamy is the same.

Oscar Wilde, Irish writer

A journey is like marriage. The certain way to be wrong is to think you control it.

John Steinbeck, US writer

I have written a book. This will come as quite a shock to some. They didn't think I could read, much less write.

George W. Bush, US President

This is the sixth book I've written, which isn't bad for a guy who's only read two.

George Burns, US comedian

Living in a vacuum sucks.

Adrienne E. Gusoff, US comedian

The difference between fiction and reality? Fiction has to make sense.

Tom Clancy, US author

I hate to advocate drugs, alcohol, violence, or insanity to anyone, but they've always worked for me.

Hunter S. Thompson, US writer

Truth titillates the imagination far less than fiction.

Marquis de Sade, French author

Literary Levity

We make our friends. We make our enemies. But God makes our next-door neighbour.

G. K. Chesterton, English writer

What can you say about a society that says God is dead and Elvis is alive?

Irv Kupcinet, US newspaper columnist

A bookstore is one of the only pieces of evidence we have that people are still thinking.

Jerry Seinfeld, US comedian

A dog teaches a boy fidelity, perseverance and to turn round three times before lying down.

Sam Levenson, US writer

Outside of a dog, a book is a man's best friend. Inside of a dog it's too dark to read.

Goucho Marx, US comedian

Somewhere on this globe, every ten seconds, there is a woman giving birth to a child. She must be found and stopped.

Sam Levenson, US writer

An intellectual snob is someone who can listen to the *William Tell Overture* and not think of *The Lone Ranger.*

Dan Rather, US journalist

Every man with a bellyful of the classics is an enemy to the human race.

Henry Miller, US writer

Life is something that happens when you can't get to sleep.

Fran Lebowitz, US writer

After an author has been dead for some time, it becomes increasingly difficult for his publishers to get a new book out of him each year.

Robert Benchley, US humorist

Advice is what we ask for when we already know the answer, but wish we didn't.

Erica Jong, US writer

The four most beautiful words in our common language: I told you so.

Gore Vidal, US writer

Facts and truth really don't have much to do with each other.

William Faulkner, US writer

I met a man at a party. He said I'm writing a novel. I said, 'Oh, really? Neither am I.'

Peter Cook, British comedian

One of the most wonderful things about life is that we must regularly stop what we are doing and devote our attention to eating.

Dr Samuel Johnson, English writer, well known for his appetite

Wit ought to be a glorious treat like caviar; never spread it about like marmalade.

Noël Coward, English playwright

Give a man a mask and he'll tell you the truth.

Oscar Wilde, Irish writer

A woman, especially, if she have the misfortune of knowing anything, should conceal it as well as she can.

Jane Austen, British author

This is a feminist bookstore. There is no humour section.

John Callahan, US humorist

He knew everything about literature except how to enjoy it.

Joseph Heller, US author

I never let schooling interfere with my education.

Mark Twain, US writer

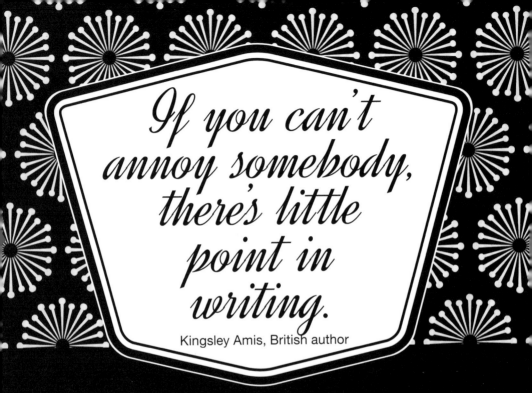

If you can't annoy somebody, there's little point in writing.

Kingsley Amis, British author

A new book smells great. An old book smells even better. An old book smells like ancient Egypt.

Ray Bradbury, US writer

Experience is a marvellous thing that enables you to recognize a mistake when you make it again.

F. P. Jones, US writer

With sixty staring me in the face, I have developed inflammation of the sentence structure and definite hardening of the paragraphs.

James Thurber, US writer

The trouble with being punctual is that nobody's there to appreciate it.

F. P. Jones, US writer

Action speaks louder than words but not nearly as often.

Mark Twain, US writer

As your attorney, it is my duty to inform you that it is not important that you understand what I'm doing or why you're paying me so much money. What's important is that you continue to do so.

US writer Hunter S. Thompson's attorney

In America, only the successful writer is important, in France all writers are important, in England no writer is important, and in Australia you have to explain what a writer is.

Geoffrey Cottrell, Australian writer

Never criticize Americans. They have the best taste that money can buy.

Miles Kington, British journalist

Sticks and stones may break my bones, but words will make me go in a corner and cry by myself for hours.

Eric Idle, British comedian

When life hands you a lemon, say, 'Oh yeah, I like lemons, what else ya got?'

Henry Rollins, US punk rock icon and writer

I like long walks, especially when they are taken by people who annoy me.

Noël Coward, English playwright

When I told the people of Northern Ireland that I was an atheist, a woman in the audience stood up and said, 'Yes, but is it the God of the Catholics or the God of the Protestants in whom you don't believe?'

Quentin Crisp, English writer

The trouble with our times is that the future is not what it used to be.

Paul Valéry, French poet

When I read something saying I've not done anything as good as *Catch-22* I'm tempted to reply, 'Who has?'

Joseph Heller, US author

I can resist everything except temptation.

Oscar Wilde, Irish writer

That woman speaks eighteen languages, and can't say No in any of them.

Dorothy Parker, US writer

The universe is a big place, perhaps the biggest.

Kilgore Trout, alter ego of
US writer Kurt Vonnegut

An original idea. That can't be too hard. The library must be full of them.

Stephen Fry, British actor and comedian

Blessed is he who expects nothing, for he shall never be disappointed.

Jonathan Swift, English writer

Well, the only way I can get a leading-man role is if I write it.

John Cleese, British actor

The surest way to make a monkey out of a man is to quote him.

Robert Benchley, US humorist

Lord, how the day passes! It's like life - so quickly when we don't watch it, and so slowly if we do.

John Steinbeck, US writer

When words are scarce they are seldom spent in vain.

William Shakespeare, English playwright

A government that robs Peter to pay Paul can always depend on the support of Paul.

George Bernard Shaw, Irish playwright

Today's public figures can no longer write their own speeches or books, and there is some evidence that they can't read them either.

Gore Vidal, US writer

A blank piece of paper is God's way of telling us how hard it is to be God.

Sidney Sheldon, US writer

> A lawyer with a briefcase can steal more than a thousand men with guns.

US screenwritter Mario Puzo in *The Godfather*

> She looked as if she had been poured into her clothes and had forgotten to say 'when'.

P. G. Wodehouse, British writer

It was a blonde. A blonde to make a bishop kick a hole in a stained glass window.

US novelist Raymond Chandler in *Farewell, My Lovely*

I don't owe a penny to a single soul – not counting tradesmen, of course.

P. G. Wodehouse, British writer

Being kissed by a man who doesn't wax his moustache is like eating an egg without salt.

Rudyard Kipling, English writer

Mr. Henry James writes fiction as if it were a painful duty.

Oscar Wilde, Irish writer

You can say any foolish thing to a dog, and the dog will give you a look that says, 'My God, you're right! I never would've thought of that!'

Dave Barry, US writer

Get your facts first, then you can distort them as you please.

Mark Twain, US writer

You teach a child to read, and he or her will be able to pass a literacy test.

George W. Bush, US President

Fashions have done more harm than revolutions.

Victor Hugo, French writer

I am the literary equivalent of a Big Mac and Fries.

Stephen King, US writer

It is my ambition to say in ten sentences what others say in a whole book.

Friedrich Nietzsche, German philosopher

It is even harder for the average ape to believe that he has descended from man.

H. L. Mencken, US journalist

I find television very educating. Every time somebody turns on the set, I go into the other room and read a book.

Groucho Marx, US comedian

Any man who can drive safely while kissing a pretty girl is simply not giving the kiss the attention it deserves.

Albert Einstein, German physicist

All women become
like their mothers.
That is their tragedy.
No man does. That's his.

Oscar Wilde, Irish writer

Literary Levity

Nothing is so good as it seems beforehand.

English writer George Eliot in *Silas Marner*

You live and learn, then die and forget it all.

Noël Coward, English playwright

'Classic': a book which people praise and don't read.

Mark Twain, US writer

From the moment I picked your book up until I laid it down, I was convulsed with laughter. Someday I intend reading it.

Groucho Marx, US comedian

This is not a novel to be tossed aside lightly. It should be thrown with great force.

Dorothy Parker, US writer

Writing is the only profession where no one considers you ridiculous if you earn no money.

Jules Renard, French author

Write something, even if it's just a suicide note.

Gore Vidal, US writer

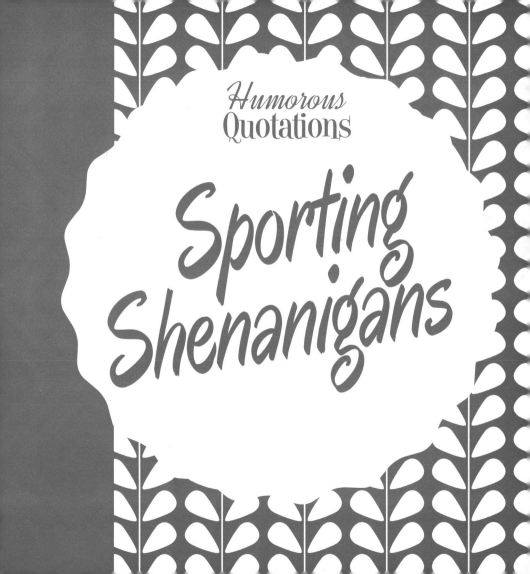

Humorous Quotations

Sporting Shenanigans

I'm one of those people who's not really turned on by baseball. My idea of a relief pitcher is one that's filled with martinis.

Dean Martin, US singer

I don't understand American football at all. It looks like all-in wrestling with crash helmets.

Sting, English musician

A hot dog at the game beats roast beef at the Ritz.

Humphrey Bogart, US actor

Baseball has the great advantage over cricket of being sooner ended.

George Bernard Shaw, Irish playwright

The first time I see a jogger smiling, I'll consider it.

Joan Rivers, US comedian

My idea of exercise is a good brisk sit.

Phyllis Diller, US comedian

I'm Jewish. I don't exercise. If God wanted us to bend over he'd put diamonds on the floor.

Joan Rivers, US comedian

I have never taken any exercise except sleeping and resting.

Mark Twain, US writer

I don't jog, it makes the ice jump right out of my glass.

David Lee Roth, US singer

I've never had major knee surgery on any other part of my body.

Winston Bennett, US basketball player

I'll fight Lloyd Honeyghan for nothing if the price is right.

Marlon Starling, US boxer

I have flabby thighs, but fortunately my stomach covers them.

Roseanne Barr, US comedian

I'll moider da bum!

US Boxer Tony Galento when asked his opinion of William Shakespeare

Sure, there have been injuries and deaths in boxing – but none of them serious.

Alan Minter, English boxer

It's not whether you get knocked down, it's whether you get up.

Vincent Lombardi, US football coach

Boxing is like jazz. The better it is, the less people appreciate it.

George Foreman, US boxer

I sorted out the team formation last night lying in bed with my wife. When your husband's as ugly as me, you'd only want to talk football in bed.

Harry Redknapp, English soccer coach

If you're in the penalty area and don't know what to do with the ball, put it in the net and we'll discuss the options later.

Bob Paisley, Liverpool soccer coach, advising his players.

So I said to my personal trainer, 'Can you teach me to do the splits?' He said, 'How flexible are you?' I said, 'Well ... I can't make Tuesdays.'

Tim Vine, British comedian

I hear Glenn Hoddle has found God, that must have been one hell of a pass.

Jasper Carrott, British comedian

Cross country skiing is great if you live in a small country.

Steven Wright, US comedian

You have to run as fast as you can just to stay where you are. If you want to get anywhere, you'll have to run much faster.

Lewis Carroll, English writer

I have often wanted to drown my troubles, but I can't get my wife to go swimming.

Jimmy Carter, US President

The reason most people play golf is to wear clothes they would not be caught dead in.

Roger Simon, US writer

I need a doctor immediately. Ring the nearest golf course.

Groucho Marx, US comedian

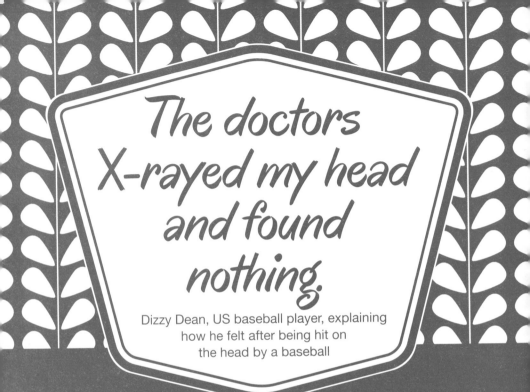

The doctors X-rayed my head and found nothing.

Dizzy Dean, US baseball player, explaining how he felt after being hit on the head by a baseball

We didn't underestimate them but they were a lot better than we thought.

Bobby Robson, England soccer coach

Being in politics is like being a football coach; you have to be smart enough to understand the game, and dumb enough to think it's important.

Eugene McCarthy, US politician

One lesson you better learn if you want to be in politics is that you never go out on a golf course and beat the President.

Lyndon B. Johnson, US President

I believe every human has a finite number of heartbeats. I don't intend to waste any of mine running around exercising.

Neil Armstrong, US astronaut

You guys line up alphabetically by height. You guys pair up in groups of three, then line up in a circle.

Bill Peterson, US football coach

I have to exercise early in the morning before my brain figures out what I am doing.

Marsha Doble, US exercise guru

There will be a game where somebody scores more than Brazil and that might be the game they lose.

Bobby Robson, England soccer coach

The reason women don't play football is because 11 of them would never wear the same outfit in public.

Phyllis Diller, US comedian

Football is a fertility festival. Eleven sperm trying to get into the egg. I feel sorry for the goalkeeper.

Bjork, Icelandic musician

Nobody in football should be called a genius. A genius is a guy like Norman Einstein.

Joe Thiesmann, US football commentator and player

They say Rome wasn't built in a day, but I wasn't in on that particular job.

Soccer coach Brian Clough, *aka* 'Old Big Head'

Sporting Shenanigans

A rooster crows only when it sees the light. Put him in the dark and he'll never crow. I have seen the light and I'm crowing.

Muhammad Ali, US boxer

Why would anyone expect him to come out smarter? He went to prison for three years, not Princeton.

Dan Duva, US boxing promoter, on Mike Tyson

I am the astronaut of boxing. Joe Louis and Jack Dempsey were just jet pilots. I'm in a world of my own.

Muhammad Ali, US boxer

I've seen better fights at a wedding.

Harry Redknapp, English soccer coach, playing down a training ground bust-up between players

213

One should always play fairly when one has the winning cards.

Oscar Wilde, Irish writer

It's good sportsmanship to not pick up lost golf balls while they are still rolling.

Mark Twain, US writer

If winning isn't everything, why do they keep score?

Vince Lombardi, US football coach

A champion is afraid of losing. Everyone else is afraid of winning.

Billie Jean King, US tennis player

Baseball is ninety per cent mental and the other half is physical.

Yogi Berra, US baseball legend

Golf is a game in which you yell fore, shoot six, and write down five.

Paul Harvey, US broadcaster

I am the greatest, I said that even before I knew I was. I figured that if I said it enough, I would convince the world that I really was the greatest.

Muhammad Ali, US boxer

Golf, like measles, should be caught young.

P. G. Wodehouse, British writer

I have a tip that can take five strokes off anyone's golf game. It's called an eraser.

Arnold Palmer, US golfing legend

I like to play in the low 70s. If it gets any hotter than that I'll stay in the bar!

Bob Hope, US comedian

I feel old when I see mousse in my opponent's hair.

Andre Agassi, US tennis veteran

My career was spluttering until I did a 360 and got headed in the right direction.

Tracy McGrady, US basketball player

McEnroe has got to sit down and work out where he stands.

Fred Perry, British tennis player

Boxing is a lot of white men watching two black men beat each other up.

Muhammad Ali, US boxer

Fast is fine, but accuracy is everything.

Wyatt Earp, US lawman and renowned gunfighter

Auto racing began 5 minutes after the second car was built.

Henry Ford, US motoring industrialist

The lead car is absolutely, truly unique, except for the one behind it which is exactly identical.

Murray Walker, British motor racing commentator

Even Napoleon had his Watergate.

Yogi Berra, US baseball legend

I know I am getting better at golf because I am hitting fewer spectators.

Gerald R. Ford, US President

Cricket is baseball on valium.

Robin Williams, US comedian

The batsman's Holding, the bowler's Willey.

Brian Johnston, British cricket commentator

He's a guy who gets up at six o'clock in the morning regardless of what time it is.

Lou Duva, US boxing coach

One of the reasons Arnie Palmer is playing so well is that, before each final round, his wife takes out his balls and kisses them. Oh my God, what have I just said.

Unattributed American commentator

He is banned from Tweeting. The next time he does that I will break both his ankles.

Richard Cockerill, English rugby union coach, bans his side from Twitter after a player revealed an injury on the social network

Rugby is a good occasion for keeping thirty bullies far from the centre of the city.

Oscar Wilde, Irish writer

Sporting Shenanigans

We have bitten off more than we can chew, but we'll chew as fast as we can.

Ian Holloway, English soccer coach

I prefer rugby to soccer. I enjoy the violence in rugby, except when they start biting each other's ears off.

Elizabeth Taylor, English actress

I never heard a minute's silence like that.

Glenn Hoddle, England soccer coach

That's great, tell him he's Pele and get him back on the pitch.

Partick Thistle soccer coach John Lambie on being informed that his concussed striker no longer knew who he was

Whenever I see an adult on a bicycle I have hope for the human race.

H. G. Wells, English writer

Playing rugby at school I once fell on a loose ball and, through ignorance and fear, held on despite a fierce pummelling. After that it took me months to convince my team-mates I was a coward.

Peter Cook, British comedian

He's certainly a very silly young man. OK, I'll say it, he's a d***head.

Australia's transport minister, Tim Pallas, is critical of F1 driver Lewis Hamilton's 'hooning' (dangerous driving) on a Melbourne street

Auto racing, bull fighting, and mountain climbing are the only real sports... all the others are games.

Ernest Hemingway, US writer

I can cry like Roger, it's just a shame I can't play like him.

Andy Murray, UK number one tennis player, after losing to Roger Federer in the final of the Australian Open

It took me seventeen years to get three thousand hits in baseball. I did it in one afternoon on the golf course.

Hank Aaron, US baseball player

I've done stupid things before when I've had too many sherbets, but nothing like this.

Welsh rugby forward Andy Powell following his arrest for driving a golf buggy down a motorway while over the alcohol limit

I told him, 'Son, what is it with you? Is it ignorance or apathy?' He said, 'Coach, I don't know and I don't care.'

Frank Layden, US basketball coach

Sporting Shenanigans

Golf is a game whose aim is to hit a very small ball into an even smaller hole, with weapons singularly ill designed for the purpose.

Winston Churchill, British Prime Minister

If you are caught on a golf course during a storm and are afraid of lightning, hold up a 1-iron. Not even God can hit a 1-iron.

Lee Trevino, American-Mexican golfer

I definitely want my son Brooklyn christened, but I don't know into what religion yet.

David Beckham, English soccer player

The only time my prayers are never answered is on the golf course.

Billy Graham, US evangelist

Golf and sex are about the only things you can enjoy without being good at.

Jimmy Demaret, US golfer

The drivers have one foot on the brake, one on the clutch, and one on the throttle.

Bob Varsha, US motor sports commentator

I owe a lot to my parents, especially my mother and father.

Greg Norman, Australian golfer

I don't need to know where the green is. Where is the golf course?

Babe Ruth, US baseball player, during a round at Pine Valley, New Jersey

I'm not saying my golf game went bad, but if I grew tomatoes, they'd come up sliced.

Lee Trevino, American-Mexican golfer

The reason the pro tells you to keep your head down is so you can't see him laughing

Phyllis Diller, US comedian

Michael Owen is a goalscorer - not a natural born one. Not yet, that takes time.

Glenn Hoddle, England soccer coach

You can sum up boxing in two words: 'You never know.'

Lou Duva, US boxing coach

Victory is fleeting. Losing is forever.

Billie Jean King, US tennis player

When I had Andre for six-and-a-half years, my main job was to keep him out of jail.

Nick Bolitieri, US tennis coach on a young tearaway called Andre Agassi

Putts get real difficult the day they hand out the money.

Lee Trevino, American-Mexican golfer

These greens are so fast I have to hold my putter over the ball and hit it with the shadow.

Sam Snead, US golfer

Sporting Shenanigans

If you watch a game, it's fun. If you play it, it's recreation. If you work at it, it's golf.

Bob Hope, US comedian

You can make a lot of money in this game. Just ask my ex-wives. Both of them are so rich that neither of their husbands work.

Lee Trevino, American-Mexican golfer

You would think that if anybody could put up a decent wall it would be China.

Terry Venables, English soccer coach

His pace is deceptive - he's slower than you think.

Bill Shankly, Liverpool soccer coach

241

Everyone has a plan 'til they get punched in the mouth.

Mike Tyson, US boxer

The older I get, the better I used to be.

Lee Trevino, American-Mexican golfer

You don't have to have been a horse to be a jockey.

Arigo Saachi, Italy soccer coach, on being a manager

Beckenbauer really has gambled all his eggs.

Ron Atkinson, English soccer coach, on the tactics of the German team

Playing polo is like trying to play golf during an earthquake.

Sylvester Stallone, US actor

If you think it's hard to meet new people, try picking up the wrong golf ball.

Jack Lemmon, US actor

Give me golf clubs, fresh air and a beautiful partner, and you can keep the clubs and the fresh air.

Jack Benny, US comedian

The slow motion replay doesn't show how fast the ball was travelling.

Richard Benaud, Australian cricket commentator

That black cloud is coming from the direction the wind is blowing, now the wind is coming from where the black cloud is.

Ray Illingworth, English cricket coach, on cricket's obsession – weather

The man who can go into a patch of rough alone, with the knowledge that only God is watching him, and play his ball where it lies, is the man who will serve you faithfully and well.

P. G. Wodehouse, British writer

I spent a lot of money on booze, birds and fast cars. The rest I just squandered.

George Best, legendary Northern Irish soccer player

He's very fast and if he gets a yard ahead of himself nobody will catch him.

Mike Ingham, English sports commentator

And I honestly believe we can go all the way to the final ... unless someone knocks us out.

John Hollins, English soccer coach

If we played like this every week, we wouldn't be so inconsistent.

Gerry Francis, England soccer player and coach

The honey badger is an animal that lives in Africa. It's about half a metre long and it's the most fearless animal on the planet. It will take on any animal, even lions. I'm trying to think like a honey badger.

Nick Cummins, Australian rugby union winger

Juantorena opens his legs and shows his class.

David Coleman, British commentator

He's a player you only miss when he's not playing.

Graham Taylor, England soccer coach

I never play cricket. It requires one to assume such indecent postures.

Oscar Wilde, Irish writer

In the rear, the small diminutive figure of Shoaib Mohammed, who can't be much taller or shorter than he is.

Henry Blofeld, English cricket commentator

That's the fastest time ever run – but it's not as fast as the world record.

David Coleman, British commentator

Sporting Shenanigans

I'm sure our physio knows what he's doing so I'm leaving my pubic area in his hands.

Sam Thaiday, Australian rugby league forward, reveals his injury battle with osteitis pubis

Although I am not a vain person, I believe that I am the very best footballer in the whole world.

Ronaldinho, Brazilian soccer player

Always remember money isn't everything – but also remember to make a lot of it before talking such fool nonsense.

Earl Wilson, US baseball pitcher

Horse sense is the thing a horse has which keeps it from betting on people.

W. C. Fields, US comedian

The three toughest fighters I've ever been up against were Sugar Ray Robinson, Sugar Ray Robinson and Sugar Ray Robinson. I fought Sugar so many times, I'm surprised I'm not diabetic!

US boxing champion Jake LaMotta

I'm really exciting. I smile a lot, I win a lot, and I'm really sexy.

US tennis champ Serena Williams gives a modest appraisal of herself

Showing off is the fool's idea of glory.

Bruce Lee, US actor and kung fu specialist

Both sides scored a couple of goals, and both sides have conceded a couple of goals.

Dave Bassett, English soccer commentator

The score never interested me, only the game.

Mae West, US actress

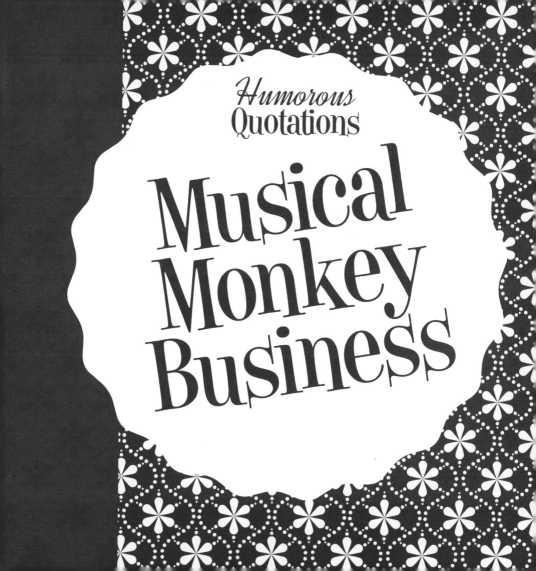

Humorous
Quotations

Musical
Monkey
Business

I do live like a rock star but it's not as great as it sounds. It's a lot of travelling.

Ron White, US comedian

Ambition is a dream with a V8 engine.

Elvis Presley, US singer

Money doesn't talk, it swears.

Bob Dylan, US singer-songwriter

You have Van Gogh's ear for music.

Billy Wilder, Austrian screenwriter and director

I got nasty habits; I take tea at three.

Mick Jagger, English singer

Musical Monkey Business

An agent is a person who is sore because an actor gets ninety per cent of what they make.

Elton John, English rock star

Music is everybody's possession. It's only publishers who think that people own it.

John Lennon, English musician

Beware the lollipop of mediocrity. Lick it once and you'll suck for ever.

Brian Wilson, The Beach Boys

Hell is full of musical amateurs.

George Bernard Shaw, Irish playwright

We don't like their sound, and guitar music is on the way out.

Decca Record Company's explanation for rejecting the Beatles in 1962

Reporter to the Beatles during their first US tour

How do you find America?

Ringo Starr

Turn left at Greenland.

Musical Monkey Business

Everyone talks about rock these days; the problem is they forget about the roll.

Keith Richards, English guitarist

Rock and roll: music for the neck downwards.

Keith Richards, English guitarist

If you had been singing like this 2,000 years ago, people would have stoned you.

Simon Cowell, *The X Factor*

Do I listen to pop music because I'm miserable or am I miserable because I listen to pop music?

John Cusack, US actor

Darling, my attitude is I'm doing everything with everyone.

Freddie Mercury, English singer

All is fair in love and songwriting.

Norah Jones, US singer-songwriter

Elvis may have been the king of rock'n'roll, but I am the queen.

Early US rock'n'roll legend Little Richard

Olivia Newton-John - Australia's gift to insomniacs. It's nothing but the blonde singing the bland.

Minnie Riperton, US singer

If you tried to give rock'n'roll another name you might call it Chuck Berry.

John Lennon, English musician

Definition of rock journalism: people who can't write, doing interviews with people who can't think, in order to prepare articles for people who can't read.

Frank Zappa, US musician

If Beethoven had been killed in a plane crash at the age of 22, it would have changed the history of music... and of aviation.

Tom Stoppard, British playwright

Composers shouldn't think. It interferes with their plagiarism.

Howard Dietz, US librettist

Musical Monkey Business

All the good music has already been written by people with wigs and stuff.

Frank Zappa, US musician

We believed that anything that was worth doing was worth overdoing.

Steven Tyler, Aerosmith

If anyone has conducted a Beethoven performance, and then doesn't have to go to an osteopath, then there's something wrong.

Simon Rattle, English conductor

Don't criticize what you don't understand, son. You never walked in that man's shoes.

Elvis Presley, US singer

Beethoven's last quartets were written by a deaf man and should only be listened to by a deaf man.

Thomas Beecham, British conductor and impresario

Musical Monkey Business

To get your playing more forceful, hit the drums harder.

Keith Moon, The Who

I understand the inventor of the bagpipes was inspired when he saw a man carrying an indignant, asthmatic pig under his arm. Unfortunately, the manmade sound never equalled the purity of the sound achieved by the pig.

Alfred Hitchcock, English director

I never thought I was wasted, but I probably was.

Keith Richards, English guitarist

I love to sing, and I love to drink scotch. Most people would rather hear me drink scotch.

George Burns, US comedian

Musical Monkey Business

It's not music.
It's a disease.

US musician Mitch Miller on rock'n'roll

One good thing about music, when it hits you, you feel no pain.

Bob Marley, Jamaican musician

When I was a little boy, I told my dad, 'When I grow up, I want to be a musician.' My dad said, 'You can't do both, Son.'

Chet Atkins, US guitarist

I wake up: I am mental, I go to bed and I am mental, I am mental within my dreams, I am mental within my normal state, I'm out of my mind.

Joey Jordison of Slipknot

Will the people in the cheaper seats clap your hands? And the rest of you, if you'll just rattle your jewellery.

John Lennon, English musician

Get up from that piano. You hurtin' its feelings.

Jelly Roll Morton, US jazz pianist

I'm not God but if I were God, three quarters of you would be girls, and the rest would be pizza and beer.

Axl Rose of Guns n' Roses

I'm not saying I'm gonna change the world, but I guarantee that I will spark the brain that will change the world.

Tupac Shakur, US rapper

I'd rather have a bottle in front of me than a frontal lobotomy.

Slogan of Stiff Records, originally by Dorothy Parker

Last night at Carnegie Hall, Jack Benny played Mendelssohn. Mendelssohn lost.

Harold C. Schonberg, US music critic

Convicts are the best audience I ever played for.

Johnny Cash, US musician

I don't know anything about music. In my line you don't have to.

Elvis Presley, US singer

To live outside the law, you must be honest.

Bob Dylan, US singer-songwriter

I'm forever near a stereo saying, 'What is this GARBAGE?' And the answer is always the Red Hot Chili Peppers.

Nick Cave, Australian singer-songwriter

Liam's like a man with a fork in a world of soup.

British musician Noel Gallagher of Oasis on his wayward brother

Every time I see Bono in those big fly glasses and tight leather pants I just can't hack it. I can't see that as solving the world's problems. He's crushing his testicles in tight trousers for world peace.

John Lydon, (Johnny Rotten) of The Sex Pistols

Anyone who thinks they're happy should really see a doctor, because there is no reason to be happy.

Marilyn Manson, US rock musician

Success is having to worry about every damn thing in the world, except money.

Johnny Cash, US musician

> *You could listen to Woody Guthrie songs and actually learn how to live ...*
>
> Bob Dylan, US singer-songwriter

> *Don't try to explain it, just sell it.*
>
> Colonel Tom Parker, manager of Elvis Presley

I just can't believe that anyone would start a band just to be cool and have chicks. I just can't believe it.

Kurt Cobain of Nirvana

To achieve great things, two things are needed: a plan, and not quite enough time.

Leonard Bernstein, US composer

Writing about music is like dancing about architecture

English singer-songwriter Elvis Costello puts down all music journalists

People are wrong when they say opera is not what it used to be. It is what it used to be. That is what's wrong with it.

Noël Coward, English playwright

I like your opera. I think I will set it to music.

Ludwig van Beethoven, German composer

I don't recall being born, perhaps it happened during one of my blackouts.

Jim Morrison of The Doors

Music is the soundtrack to the crappy movie that is my life.

Chris Rock, US comedian

If you give me the chance, I'll destroy America for you.

John Lydon (Johnny Rotten) of The Sex Pistols

I wanted to be the first woman to burn her bra, but it would have taken the fire department four days to put it out.

Dolly Parton, US musician and actress

I think Mick Jagger would be astounded and amazed if he realized that to many people he is not a sex symbol, but a mother image.

David Bowie, British rock star

It's a good thing I was born a girl, otherwise I'd be a drag queen.

Dolly Parton, US musician and actress

All I can be is me — whoever that is.

Bob Dylan, US singer-songwriter

Being noticed can be a burden. Jesus got himself crucified because he got himself noticed. So I disappear a lot.

Bob Dylan, US singer-songwriter

Keith Moon, God rest his soul, once drove his car through the glass doors of a hotel, driving all the way up to the reception desk, got out and asked for the key to his room.

Pete Townshend of The Who

The musician is perhaps the most modest of animals, but he is also the proudest. It is he who invented the sublime art of ruining poetry.

Erik Satie, French composer

I told people I was a drummer before I even had a set: I was a mental drummer.

Keith Moon, The Who

Rhythm is something you either have or don't have, but when you have it, you have it all over.

Elvis Presley, US singer

Man, I was tame compared to what they do now. Are you kidding? I didn't do anything but just jiggle.

Elvis Presley, US singer

On stage I make love to twenty five thousand people; and then I go home alone.

Janis Joplin, US musician

Anyone who thinks they're sexy needs their head checked.

Jarvis Cocker of Pulp

I'm not offended by all the dumb blonde jokes because I know I'm not dumb... and I also know that I'm not blonde.

Dolly Parton, US musician and actress

I couldn't wait to change my name anyway, because I'm not too fond of the name Reginald. It's a very kind of 50s English name.

Elton John, English rock star

You'd be surprised how much it costs to look this cheap!

Dolly Parton, US musician and actress

Musical Monkey Business

Why do they cover Paul's songs but never mine?

Yoko Ono, wife of John Lennon

It's better to burn out than fade away.

Neil Young, US musician

I'd rather be dead than cool.

Kurt Cobain of Nirvana

I can't listen to that much Wagner. I start getting the urge to conquer Poland.

Woody Allen, US writer-director

I love Wagner, but the music I prefer is that of a cat hung up by its tail outside a window and trying to stick to the panes of glass with its claws.

Charles-Pierre Baudelaire, French poet

> If I had to do my life over, I would change every single thing that I have done.

Ray Davies, The Kinks

> Anything that is too stupid to be spoken is sung.

Voltaire, French writer

He has a woman's name and wears makeup. How original.

US rock star Alice Cooper on Marilyn Manson

Mr Wagner has beautiful moments but bad quarters of an hour.

Gioacchino Antonio Rossini, Italian composer

Musical Monkey Business

If I wasn't a musician I don't know. I'd be God, maybe? That would be a good job.

Liam Gallagher, British musician

After Rossini dies, who will there be to promote his music?

Richard Wagner, German composer

We are better than anyone, ain't we? Except for the Eagles - the Eagles are better than us.

Sid Vicious, The Sex Pistols

Wagner's music is better than it sounds.

Mark Twain, US writer

You see, what sounds to you like a big load of trashy noise ... is in fact ... the brilliant music of a genius ... myself.

US musician Iggy Pop on his uniquely trashy brand of rock'n'roll

Too many pieces of music finish too long after the end.

Igor Stravinsky, Russian composer

Rock and menopause do not mix.

Stevie Nicks, US singer-songwriter

I'd rather be dead than singing 'Satisfaction' when I'm forty-five.

Mick Jagger, English singer

I look just like the girls next door... if you happen to live next door to an amusement park.

Dolly Parton, US musician and actress

Musical Monkey Business

I've always wanted the sound of Muddy Waters' early records - only louder.

Eric Clapton, English guitarist

I've only got one solo, but it's a doozy!

Angus Young, AC/DC's explosive lead guitarist, on his playing style

Music makes one feel so romantic – at least it always gets on one's nerves – which is the same thing nowadays.

Oscar Wilde, Irish writer

I've been through more cold turkeys than there are freezers.

Keith Richards, English guitarist

I know [canned music] makes chickens lay more eggs and factory workers produce more. But how much more can they get out of you in an elevator?

Victor Borge, Danish-American musician and comedian

I opened the door for a lot of people, and they just ran through and left me holding the knob.

Bo Diddley, US rhythm and blues musician, on his innovative blues/rock sound being stolen by the white musicians of the early 60s

I do maintain that if your hair is wrong, your entire life is wrong.

Morrissey, The Smiths

When I went to school, they asked me what I wanted to be when I grew up. I wrote down 'happy'. They told me I didn't understand the assignment; I told them they didn't understand life.

John Lennon, English musician

The reason I'm running for President is because I can't be Bruce Springsteen.

Barack Obama, US President

Society has traditionally always tried to find scapegoats for its problems. Well, here I am.

Marilyn Manson, US rock musician

An unalterable and unquestioned law of the musical world required that the German text of French operas sung by Swedish artists should be translated into Italian for the clearer understanding of English-speaking audiences.

Edith Wharton, US novellist

How wonderful opera would be if there were no singers.

Gioacchino Antonio Rossini, Italian composer

A lot of my audience are in their fifties. But they want me to pretend to continue to be pretending.

Pete Townshend of The Who

I remember when the candle shop burned down. Everyone stood around singing 'Happy Birthday'.

Steven Wright, US comedian

I've never had a message for anyone in my entire life. Except maybe to give out my room number.

AC/DC's Bon Scott on the social responsibility of rock lyricists

Brass bands are all very well in their place - outdoors and several miles away.

Thomas Beecham, British conductor and impresario

311

Musical Monkey Business

I'm tired of me, I'm sure the public is as well.

Michael Stipe of R.E.M. on overexposure

I suppose on some deep and profound level the evening would seem incomplete to me without three minutes of howling.

US musician Warren Zevon explaining the origins of 'Werewolves of London'

I don't like country music, but I don't mean to denigrate those who do. And for the people who like country music, denigrate means 'put down'.

Bob Newhart, US comedian and actor

I'd like to get something together - like a Handel, Bach, Muddy Waters, flamenco-type of thing. If I could get *that* sound, I'd be happy.

Jimi Hendrix, US guitarist

All music is folk music. I ain't never heard no horse sing a song.

Louis Armstrong, US jazz musician

Don't ever call me your drummer again ...You're my singer!

Rolling Stones drummer Charlie Watts after punching a drunk Mick Jagger in the face

The difference between a violin and a viola is that a viola burns longer.

Victor Borge, Danish-American musician and comedian

Musical Monkey Business

... everyone was using tiny brushes and doing watercolours, while Jimi Hendrix was painting galactic scenes in Cinemascope.

Carlos Santana, US guitarist

I'm stupid, I'm ugly, I'm dumb, I smell. Did I mention I'm stupid?

Eminem, US rapper

I got rabies shots for biting the head off a bat but that's OK - the bat had to get Ozzy shots.

Ozzy Osbourne, Black Sabbath

A lot of truth is said in jest.

Eminem, US rapper

Husbands are like fires - they go out when they're left unattended.

Cher, US singer

The trouble with some women is that they get all excited about nothing - and then marry him.

Cher, US singer

Everyone got it wrong. I said I was into porn again, not born again.

Billy Idol, English rock musician

I feel like a million tonight – but one at a time.

Bette Midler, US singer and actress

Musical Monkey Business

The hippies wanted peace and love. We wanted Ferraris, blondes and switchblades.

Alice Cooper, US rock star

Guess what, I might be the first hippie pinup girl.

Janis Joplin, US musician

Humorous Quotations

Classic One-Liners

Infamy, infamy! They've all got it in for me!

English actor Kenneth Williams in *Carry On Cleo*

Maybe, just once, someone will call me 'Sir' without adding, 'You're making a scene.'

Homer Simpson, cartoon character

I can still enjoy sex at 75 ... I live at 76, so it's no distance.

Bob Monkhouse, English comedian

Sex at age 90 is like trying to shoot pool with a rope.

George Burns, US comedian

Conjunctivitis dot com ... now there's a site for sore eyes.

Tim Vine, British comedian

Oh, so they have internet on computers now!

Homer Simpson, cartoon character

I have had a lovely evening - unfortunately, this wasn't it.

Groucho Marx, US comedian

Never moon a werewolf!

Mike Binder, US film director

You can't have everything. Where would you put it?

Steven Wright, US comedian

I am an expert on electricity. My father occupied the chair of applied electricity at the state prison.

W. C. Fields, US comedian

A woman drove me to drink and I didn't even have the decency to thank her.

W. C. Fields, US comedian

My wife had a go at me last night. She said, 'You'll drive me to my grave.' I had the car out in thirty seconds.

Tommy Cooper, English comedian

Always get married in the morning. That way if it doesn't work out, you haven't wasted the whole day.

Mickey Rooney, US actor

Classic One-Liners

I'm on a whisky diet, I've lost three days already.

Tommy Cooper, English comedian

I never forget a face, but in your case I'll be glad to make an exception.

Groucho Marx, US comedian

Brevity is the soul of lingerie.

Dorothy Parker, US writer

My dog was barking at everyone the other day. Still what can you expect from a cross-breed.

Tim Vine, British comedian

If all the young ladies who attended the Yale prom were laid end to end, no one would be the least surprised.

Dorothy Parker, US writer

'You remind me of a pepper-pot.'

Garry Kasparov, Russian chess grandmaster

'I'll take that as a condiment.'

Peter Kay, British comedian

I had a meal last night,
I ordered everything
in French ... surprised
everybody, it was a
Chinese restaurant.

Tommy Cooper, English comedian

*Never have children,
only grandchildren.*

Gore Vidal, US writer

Tonight we'll be talking to a car designer who's crossed Toyota with Quasimodo and come up with the Hatchback of Notre Dame.

Ronnie Corbett, British comedian

My mother-in-law has come round to our house at Christmas seven years running. This year we're having a change, we're going to let her in.

Les Dawson, British comedian

True friends stab you in the front.

Oscar Wilde, Irish writer

I don't want to achieve immortality through my work. I want to achieve it through not dying.

Woody Allen, US writer-director

If God wanted us to fly, he would have given us air tickets.

Mel Brooks, US director

When I was a boy, the Dead Sea was only sick.

George Burns, US comedian

If God had wanted us to vote, he would have given us candidates.

Jay Leno, US comedian and chat show host

I haven't spoken to my mother-in-law for eighteen months. I don't like to interrupt her.

Ken Dodd, British comedian

My mother-in-law fell down a wishing well. I was amazed — I never knew they worked.

Les Dawson, British comedian

I am not afraid of death, I just don't want to be there when it happens.

Woody Allen, US writer-director

I intend to live forever. So far, so good.

Steven Wright, US comedian

The way forwards is backwards.

Dave Sexton, English soccer coach

If Shaw and Einstein couldn't beat death, what chance have I got? Practically none.

Mel Brooks, US director

A cement mixer has collided with a prison van. Motorists are asked to look out for 16 hardened criminals.

Ronnie Corbett, British comedian

I'd stay away from Ecstasy; this is a drug so strong it makes white people think they can dance!

Lenny Henry, British comedian

When I first said I wanted to be a comedian, everyone laughed. They're not laughing now.

Bob Monkhouse, English comedian

I'm not upset about my divorce. I'm only upset I'm not a widow.

Roseanne Barr, US comedian, on Tom Arnold

I've done my bit for motion pictures; I've stopped making them.

Liberace, US musician

I just got back from a pleasure trip. I took my mother-in-law to the airport.

Henny Youngman, British-American comedian

What do I wear in bed? Why, Chanel No. 5, of course.

Marilyn Monroe, US actress

What do you call a blonde with brains? A labrador.

Lee Mack, British comedian

I failed to make the chess team because of my height.

Woody Allen, US writer-director

It is not enough to succeed. Others must fail.

Gore Vidal, US writer

A three-legged dog walks into a saloon in the Old West. He sidles up to the bar and says: 'I'm looking for the man who shot my paw!'

Tim Vine, British comedian

If you come to a fork in the road, take it.

Yogi Berra, US baseball legend

I want to die like my father, peacefully in his sleep, not screaming and terrified, like his passengers.

Bob Monkhouse, English comedian

Always go to other people's funerals, otherwise they won't come to yours.

Yogi Berra, US baseball legend

345

I can always tell when my mother-in-law's coming to stay ... the mice throw themselves on the traps.

Les Dawson, British comedian

Where there's a will - there's a relative!

Ricky Gervais, English comedian and actor

I wanted to do something nice so I bought my mother-in-law a chair. Now they won't let me plug it in.

Henny Youngman, British-American comedian

If life was fair, Elvis would be alive and all the impersonators would be dead.

Johnny Carson, US comedian and TV host

I've just been on a once-in-a-lifetime holiday. I tell you what ... never again!

Tim Vine, British comedian

Mail your packages early so the post office can lose them in time for Christmas.

Johnny Carson, US comedian and TV host

A foolproof plan for not getting a job — in the event of an interview, wear flip-flops.

Alan Davies, British comedian

If you want to make God laugh, tell him about your plans.

Woody Allen, US writer-director

If somebody in the crowd spits at you, you've just got to swallow it.

Gary Lineker, soccer player and broadcaster

Why does a woman work ten years to change a man's habits and then complain that he's not the man she married?

Barbra Streisand, US singer and actress

I used to be Snow White, but I drifted.

Mae West, US actress

Those are my principles, and if you don't like them ... well, I have others.

Groucho Marx, US comedian

Doctor, doctor, I think I am a pair of curtains.

Pull yourself together, man.

Doctor, doctor, I think I am a bridge.

What's come over you? Several cars, a large truck and a bus.

Doctor, Doctor, I can't stop my hands shaking!

Do you drink a lot? Not really, I spill most of it!

I remember the shouts of 'Scab!' as my father went to work during the great dermatologists' strike.

Harry Hill, British comedian

She said she was approaching forty, and I couldn't help wondering from what direction.

Bob Hope, US comedian

You go Uruguay, and I'll go mine.

Groucho Marx in *Animal Crackers*

When I'm good I'm very, very good, but when I'm bad, I'm better.

Mae West, US actress

Doctor, doctor, I feel like a pack of cards.

I'll deal with you later.

Doctor, doctor, my son has just swallowed a roll of film.

Let's hope nothing develops.

Doctor, Doctor, every time I drink a cup of coffee I get this stabbing pain in my eye!

I suggest you take the spoon out!

If love is the answer, could you please rephrase the question?

Lily Tomlin, US actress

He's the kind of man a woman would have to marry to get rid of.

Mae West, US actress

Two eskimos sitting in a kayak were chilly; but when they lit a fire in the craft, it sank, proving once and for all that you can't have your kayak and heat it too.

Tim Vine, British comedian

Go, and never darken my towels again.

Groucho Marx, US comedian

357

Bigamy is the only crime where two rites make a wrong.

Bob Hope, US comedian

I don't care what you say about me.
Just be sure to spell my name wrong.

Barbra Streisand, US singer and actress

My mom said the only reason men are alive is for lawn care and vehicle maintenance.

Tim Allen, US comedian

Never eat more than you can lift.

Miss Piggy, muppet

Weather forecast for tonight: dark.

George Carlin, US comedian

Life is full of misery, loneliness, and suffering – and it's all over much too soon.

Woody Allen, US writer-director

If it's the Psychic Network why do they need a phone number?

Robin Williams, US comedian

In America, we like everyone to know about the good work we're doing anonymously.

Jay Leno, US comedian and chat show host

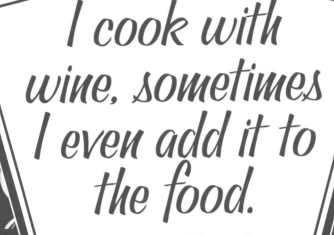

I cook with wine, sometimes I even add it to the food.

W. C. Fields, US comedian

It is funnier to bend things than to break them.

W. C. Fields, US comedian

There are two seasons in Scotland: June and winter.

Billy Connolly, Scottish comedian

I was the *kid next door's* imaginary friend.

Emo Philips, US entertainer and comedian

A sure cure for seasickness is to sit under a tree.

Spike Milligan, Anglo-Irish comedian

Multi-storey car parks – they are just wrong on so many levels.

Tim Vine, British comedian

All generalizations are false, including this one.

Mark Twain, US writer

When I invite a woman to dinner, I expect her to look at my face. That's the price she has to pay.

George S. Kaufman, US playwright

Anyone who says he can see through women is missing a lot.

Groucho Marx, US comedian

I don't like all this fresh air. I'm from Los Angeles; I don't trust any air I can't see.

Bob Hope, US comedian

Go to Heaven for the climate, Hell for the company.

Mark Twain, US writer

A tom cat hijacked a plane, stuck a pistol into the pilot's ribs and demanded, 'Take me to the Canaries.'

Bob Monkhouse, English comedian

He taught me housekeeping; when I divorce I keep the house.

Zsa Zsa Gabor, American-Hungarian actress

Don't stay in bed, unless you can make money in bed.

George Burns, US comedian

It's so long since I've had sex I've forgotten who ties up who.

Joan Rivers, US comedian

I do wish we could chat longer, but I'm having an old friend for dinner.

Hannibal Lecter in *The Silence of the Lambs*

Is Elizabeth Taylor fat? Her favorite food is seconds.

Joan Rivers, US comedian

The only difference between me and a madman is that I'm not mad.

Salvador Dalí, Spanish artist

Happiness is having a large, loving, caring, close-knit family in another city.

George Burns, US comedian

All I ask is the chance to prove, that money can't make me happy.

Spike Milligan, Anglo-Irish comedian

I'm living so far beyond my income that we may almost be said to be living apart.

E. E. Cummings, US poet

Women might be able to fake orgasms. But men can fake a whole relationship.

Sharon Stone, US actress

A lie gets halfway around the world before the truth has a chance to get its pants on.

Winston Churchill, British Prime Minister

A narcissist is someone better-looking than you are.

Gore Vidal, US writer

If the facts don't fit the theory, change the facts.

Albert Einstein, German physicist

Show me a woman who doesn't feel guilty and I'll show you a man.

Erica Jong, US writer

People who think they know everything are a great annoyance to those of us who do.

Isaac Asimov, US author

Happiness is good health and a bad memory.

Ingrid Bergman, Swedish film star

Write drunk; edit sober.

Ernest Hemingway, US writer

Everybody's got to believe in something. I believe I'll have another beer.

W. C. Fields, US comedian

375

I never miss a chance to have sex or appear on television.

Gore Vidal, US writer

To err is human, but it feels divine.

Mae West, US actress

Fill what's empty, empty what's full, and scratch where it itches.

The Duchess of Windsor, when asked what was the secret of a long and happy life

A good deed never goes unpunished.

Gore Vidal, US writer

There is more stupidity than hydrogen in the universe, and it has a longer shelf life.

Frank Zappa, US musician

I am at peace with God. My conflict is with Man.

Charlie Chaplin, British comic actor

The nice thing about being a celebrity is that if you bore people they think it's their fault.

Henry Kissinger, US diplomat

Men are so willing to respect anything that bores them.

Marilyn Monroe, US actress

Be nice to people on your way up because you meet them on your way down.

Jimmy Durante, US comedian

Formula for success: rise early, work hard, strike oil.

J. Paul Getty, US industrialist

Some cause happiness wherever they go; others, whenever they go.

Oscar Wilde, Irish writer

Sometimes the road less travelled is less travelled for a reason.

Jerry Seinfeld, US comedian

Tragedy is when I cut my finger. Comedy is when you walk into an open sewer and die.

Mel Brooks, US director

Do not try to live forever. You will not succeed.

George Bernard Shaw, Irish playwright

If you can count your money, you don't have a billion dollars.

J. Paul Getty, US industrialist

I have never killed a man, but I have read many obituaries with great pleasure.

Clarence Darrow, US Civil Liberties Lawyer

George Bernard Shaw to Winston Churchill:

I am enclosing two tickets to the first night of my new play. Bring a friend... if you have one.

Churchill in response:

Cannot possibly attend first night. Will attend second... if there is one.